CONTENTS

CONTENTS

I Walk Alone

(Cammino da Solo)

I walk alone...
....yeah, with nobody else!
I walk alone.
I prefer to be by myself!

"The Don"
21.10.2022

How Long Has It Been Since You Played the Piano?
(Quanto Tempo è Passato da Quando hai Suonato il Piano?)

Yeah...
...how long has it been since you sat down in front of a keyboard?
Yeah...
...how long has it been since you've looked at the keyboard?
Yeah...
...how long has it been since you've touched those keys?
Yeah...
...how long has it been since you ran your fingers up & down those black & white keys?
Yeah...
...how long has it been since you played those black & whites?
Yeah...
...how long has it been since you played Mozart?
Yeah...
...how long has it been since you played the love of your life...
...Beethoven?
Yeah...
...how long has it been since you played your mentor & inspiration of your life...
...Villa Lobos?
Yeah...
...how long has it been since you played the piano?
Yeah...
...how long has it been since?
Yeah...
...how long has it been since?
Yeah...
...how long has it been since?
Yeah...
...how long has it been since?

"The Don"
24.10.2022

SHE CAN NEVER FORGET THAT

(Non Si Può Mai Dimenticarlo)

I offered my outstretched hand when she was on the floor.
She can never forget that!

She took my hand.
She can never forget that!

She said, *"You're my knight in shining armour".*
She can never forget that!

She said, *"You saved me when no one else would".*
She can never forget that!

She said, *"You are my Saviour".*
She can never forget that!

We wrote poetry together & made you immortal.
She can never forget that!

She said, *"I LO♥E you!"*
She can never forget that!

SHE CAN NEVER FORGET THAT

"The Don"
24.10.2022

The "Friend Zone"

(La "Zona Amica")

Oh no....
.....NO!
Don't put me in the *"Friend Zone"*!
Shit, shit shit!
I'm in the *"Friend Zone"*!
FUUUUUUUUCK NOOOOOOOOO!
NOT the *"Friend Zone"*!
"You are now entering the *"Friend Zone"*, from which there is NO escaping"!
Once inside the *"Friend Zone"* there is NO way out.
It is a *"lifetime"* sentence.
You will be imprisoned in the *"Friend Zone"* FOREVER!
You will NEVER get out once inside the *"Friend Zone"*.
Escape is FUTILE from the *"Friend Zone"*.

The only way to escape from the *"Friend Zone"* is to *"BLOW it up"*!
This is EXTREMELY dangerous!
For in the process of destroying the *"Friend Zone"*...
...you could destroy yourself!
But this is the risk you take...
...if you EVER want to leave the *"Friend Zone"*.

If you are in or find yourself entering the *"Friend Zone"*...
...then, *"good luck"*!
You will need it to escape the *"Friend Zone"*.

"Ahhhhhhhhhhhhhhhhhhhhhhhhhhhh!"
"Let me out of HERE!!!!!!!!"

"I don't want to be in here!"

"I don't want to be in the "Friend Zone"!"

"The Don"
25.10 2022

There's Something Going on Here

(C'è Qualcosa che sta Succedendo Qui)

There's something going on here...
...but you don't know what it is?
Do you?
There is...
...confusion,
...collusion,
...disillusion,
...illusion.

There's something going on here...
...but you don't know what it is?
Do you?

There is...
...connection,
...affection,
...dejection,
...rejection.

There's something going on here...
...but you don't know what it is?
Do you?

There is...
...laughter,
...fun,
...happiness,
...sadness.

There's something going on here...
...but you don't know what it is?
Do you?

There is...
...LO♥E!

There's something going on here...
...but you don't know what it is?
Do you?

"You walk into the room with your pencil in your hand
You see somebody naked and you say, "Who is that man?"
You try so hard but you don't understand
Just what you will say when you get home
Because something is happening here but you don't know what it is
Do you, Mr. Jones?"

"Ballad of a Thin Man"
Written & performed by: Bob Dylan

"The Don"
27.10.2022

SECRET AGENT MAN

(Agente Segreto Uomo)

Beware!
Take care!
Look out!
Danger is about!
He's *illusive.*
He's an *enigma.*
He's a *mystery.*
He's a *"Danger Man"*!
He's an *"International man of mystery".*
He's a *"Secret Agent Man".*

Don't *get involved.*
Don't *fall for his charms.*
Don't *become entranced with his charisma.*
Don't *fall for his witty repartee.*
Don't get *caught in his trap.*
Don't get *ensnared in his net.*
Don't get *stuck in the web that he weaves.*
Whatever you do...
...don't *fall in LO❤E with him.*
Because...
...he's an *"International man of mystery".*
He's a *"Secret Agent Man".*

He is very DANGEROUS!

"I'm a man who leads a life of danger.
To everyone I meet I am a stranger
Trouble is my number & danger is my game"
Odds are I won't live to see tomorrow.

Secret Agent Man
Secret Agent Man"

"Secret Agent Man"

Performed by: Johnny Rivers
Composed by: P. F. Sloan & Steve Barri

"The Don"
31.10.2022

Nobody Here Gets Out Alive

(Nessuno Qui ne Esce Vivo)

Don't *struggle*.
Don't *fight it*.
Don't *run away*.
Don't *worry*.
Don't *fret*.
Don't *panic*.
Don't *fear it*.
Because...
...nobody here gets out alive.

You can't *escape it*.
You can't *postpone it*.
You can't *negotiate it*.
You can't *deny it*.
You can't *defy it*.
You can't *escape it*.
Because...
...nobody here gets out alive.

Accept your *fate*.
Accept your *destiny*.
Accept your *future*.
Accept your *ending*.
Accept your *life*.
Accept your *death*.
Because...
...nobody here gets out alive.

Nobody here gets out alive.

Nobody here gets out alive.

Nobody here gets out alive.

Nobody here gets out alive.

"The Don"
02.11.2022

I Am a Fraud

(Sono Uno frode)

I *lie.*
I *manipulate.*
I *fake it.*
I *elaborate.*
I *fabricate.*
I *deceive.*
I am a fraud.

I cannot be *trusted.*
I cannot be *believed.*
I cannot be *counted on.*
I cannot be *relied upon.*
I cannot be a *friend.*
I cannot be a *LO♥ER.*
I am a fraud.

That's right...
...*I am a fraud.*

I'm telling you straight...
...*I am a fraud.*

"The Don"
02.11.2022

All Because of

Pussy & Cock

(Tutto a Causa della Figa e del Cazzo)

All because of pussy & cock we can't be friends.
I want her pussy but she doesn't want my cock.

She doesn't care that someone actually loves her.
LO❤E is a dirty word to her!
Apparently, it's all about cock!
I can't do anything about it.
I don't have the *"right "*cock!

Although she prefers the word *"dick".*

"The Don"
04.11.2022

 The Ying & the Yang
at the Same Time
(Lo Ying e lo Yang allo Stesso Tempo)

What a *confusion!*
What a *mess!*
I don't know whether I'm *Ying* or *Yang.*
I'm all over the place.
I am experiencing both simultaneously.
I can't separate the *Ying* from the *Yang.*
My brain is at war with itself.
One moment I'm *Ying* & the next moment I'm *Yang.*
Where am I?
Who am I?
Am I both?
Or neither?
Because...
...I am the Ying & the Yang at the same time.

Do they cancel themselves out...?
...when the *Ying* meets the *Yang*?
…when the *Ying & the Yang* exist at the same time?
Can they actually exist simultaneously?
They must.
Because...
...they are both happening to me.
...the Ying & the Yang at the same time.
Just call me...
..."YingYang"!

"The Don"
07.11.2022

I'm Vain

(Sono Vanitoso)

I'm vain as shit!
I LO❤E myself.
Is that bad?
I'm not a narcissist.
I don't think!
But I do LO❤E myself.
I do think that I'm the BEST.
Is that bad?
Yeah...
...*I'm vain.*

"I'm so vain,
I think this poem's about me!
I'm so vain.
I think this poem's about me...
... about me!
....about me!
... about me!
....about me!

"The Don"
09.11.2022

(Chiunque è Sessualmente Più Attraente di Me)

That's right!
I'm *old.*
I'm a *"has-been".*
I'm *"over the hill".*
I'm a *loser.*
I'm a *nobody.*
I'm a *nothing.*
I am *invisible.*
I am *"non-sexual".*
I am *"asexual".*
I am a *ghost.*
I *don't exist.*

So...
...anyone is more sexually attractive than me.

ANYONE IS MORE SEXUALLY ATTRACTIVE THAN ME

(Chiunque è Sessualmente Più Attraente di Me)

"The Don"
09.11.2022

Grin & Bare It

(Sorridi e Sopportalo)

Wear it.
Possess it.
Own it.
Control it.
Because there is nothing you can do but...
...grim & bare it.

Let it *flow.*
Let it *go.*
Let it *grow.*
Let it *take its course.*
Because there is nothing you can do but...
...grim & bare it.

Stand *tall.*
Be *proud.*
Be *resolute.*
Be *strong*
Because there is nothing you can do but...
...grim & bare it.

"The Don"
11.11.2022

No Longer My Friend by Association
(Non più mio Amico per Associazione)

She is no longer my friend.
I don't know why.
I haven't done anything.
I'm innocent.
Yet, she is *"Ghosting"* me.
I must no longer be her friend by association.

It's sad.
That's true.
It's a shame.
That's true.
But I fell out with a mutual friend.
So, I guess she is taking her side.
Because we are no longer friends.
Or so it seems.
So, I guess I am no longer her friend by association.

It sucks.
But that's the way things sometimes go.
People take sides.
Friends are a possession.
This is MY friend!
Since you two are no longer getting on.
I will choose a side.
I choose hers.
That's why we are no longer friends.
We are no longer friends by association.

"The Don"
23.11.2022

I Can Entertain Myself

(Posso Divertirmi)

I don't NEED anyone.
I've got everyone here with me.
Yep...
...there're ALL here.
Of course, you can't see them.
Because...
...there're all inside my HEAD!

There is...
...the philosopher,
...the poet,
...the musician,
...the "Pop Culture" guru,
...the comedian,
...the "BAD" boy,
...the "Sinner",
...the rebel,
...the anarchist,
...the ARSEHOLE,
...the "Nice" guy,
...the politician,
...the scientist
...the "Polemicist",
...the narcissist,
...the egoist.
...the "Saint",
...the "Sinner",
...and...
...the "LO❤ER",
Oh yeah...
...and...
...myself, of course.
Whoever the FUCK I am!

That's why I don't need anybody.
I can entertain myself!

And the music goes 'round my head!

"The Don"
23.11.2022

Don't Be Attracted by the Flame

(Non essere Attratto dalla Fiamma)

Don't *be allured by its colours.*
Don't be *mesmerised by its luminosity.*
Don't be *seduced by its mystery.*
Don't be *hypnotised by its beauty.*
Don't be *ensnared by its penumbra.*
Don't be *caught in its tendrils.*
Don't be *lulled by its seduction.*
Don't be *fooled by its promises.*
Bu whatever you do...
...don't *fall in LO❤E with it.*
You will be sourly disappointed.
So, don't be attracted by the flame...
But instead...
...be attached by its WARMTH!

"Fire, I'll take you to burn!
Fire, I'll take you to learn!
You're gonna burn!
You're gonna burn!
You're gonna burn, burn, burn, burn!
Burn, burn, burn, burn, burn, burn, burn!"

"Fire, I'll take you to burn!
Fire, I'll take you to learn!
Fire, I'll take you to bed!
Fire, I'll take you,
FIRE!"

"Fire" - "The Crazy World of Arthur Brown"

"The Don"
24.11.2022

(Che Casino!)

It's a *state of chaos.*
It's a *world of confusion.*
It's a *society of violence.*
It's a *humanity of ignorance.*
It's *an individual of SHAME!*
What a MESS!

How could we allow it to get to this?
Are we *blind?*
Are we *dumb?*
Are we *idiots?*
Are we *STOOOOOOOPID?*
What a MESS!

Will it EVER change?
Probably not!
It's ALWAYS been a MESS!!!!

"Society, you're a crazy breed
I hope you're not lonely without me
Society, crazy indeed
I hope you're not lonely without me"

"Society, have mercy on me
I hope you're not angry if I disagree
Society, crazy indeed
I hope you're not lonely
Without me."

"Society" – "Eddie Vedder"

"The Don"
25.11.2022

Your Feelings

(I Tuoi Sentimenti)

Your feelings are YOUR feelings & they should stay that way.
They belong to you only!
They do not belong to anybody else.
Don't make the common mistake of assuming that others share your feelings.
That they have the same feelings.
That they feel your feelings.
Because...
...they do not!
Your feelings are your feelings alone.
They belong only to you & nobody else.
This is the erroneous assumption that others have the same feelings as you.
They do not!

Do not make this mistake!

Do NOT force your feelings onto others.
This is a recipe for DISASTER!
Do not have an *"Emotional Fart"*!

If you are lucky, someone might have similar feelings to you.
If you are lucky!
All I can say is...
...good luck!

"Feelings, nothing more than feelings
Trying to forget my feelings of love
Teardrops rolling down on my face
Trying to forget my feelings of love."

"Feelings, for all my life I'll feel it
I wish I've never met you, girl
You'll never come again
Feelings, whoa, oh, oh, feelings
Whoa, oh, oh, feel it again in my arms."

"Feelings" – "Morris Albert"

"The Don"
27.11.2022

Highway to Hell

(Autostrada per L'inferno)

You're *moving fast.*
You're *gaining speed.*
You're *electrified.*
You're *turbocharged.*
You're *hurtling down that highway.*
I believe it's called, *"Highway '61".*
Isn't that where, *"All the killing is done"*?
Out on, *"Highway '61".*
"God said to Abraham kill me a son."
"Abe said, man you must be having me on?"
"Where do you want this killing done?"
"God said, out on Highway '61!"

There are no *stops light.*
There are no *off-ramps.*
It's *one straight road…*
…as far as the eye can see.
There is no *stopping allowed.*
There is no *slowing down.*
There is no *getting off.*
There is *only one speed…*
…VERY FAST!!!
The sign up ahead says *"You're on "Highway to Hell".*
"Enjoy the ride"!
Because…
…you're on the "Highway to Hell"!

"I'm on the "Highway to Hell"!
"Highway to Hell"!
"Highway to Hell"!
Someone, help me!!!!!
Because…
…I'm on the "Highway to Hell"!
I'm on the "Highway to Hell"!
"Highway to Hell"!
"Highway to Hell"!"

- "Highway to Hell" - "AC/DC"

"The Don"
28.11.2022

There's Not Another You

(Non c'è un Ultro Te)

You are the *"One & Only"*!
You are a *"One-Off"*!
You are a *"One-of-a-Kind"*!
You're are a *"Prototype"*!
You are *"V1.0"*!
You are *"Unique"*!
You are the only one in the *Universe*!
You are the only in all the *"Multiverses"*!
You are the only *"one"*!
There is no other *"You"*!
There is no else like *"You"*!
There is not another you!

So...
...I'm humbled I got to know you!

"The Don"
28.11.2022

Practising to be Alone

(Esercitarsi per essere Soli)

I get asked a lot,
"What are you doing with your life now?"
I say…
…*"I'm practising to be alone!"*

Another question I also get asked very often is,
"What work do you do?"
I say that…
"I'm practising to be alone!"

People quite often ask me,
"What are you going to doing with your future?
"Do you have any plans?"
I say that…
…*"I'm practising to be alone!"*

"Only the lonely
Only the lonely
Only the lonely

There goes my baby
There goes my heart
They're gone forever
So far apart
But only the lonely

Only the lonely
Only the lonely
Only the lonely"

-"Only the Lonely" – "Roy Orbison"

"The Don"
28.11.2022

In Your Head

(Nella tua Testa)

Your....
...Subjectivity.
...Objectively.
...Hatred.
...Friendship.
...Honour.
...Loyalty.
...Thoughts.
...Ideals.
...Purity.
...Society.
Your…
...Sadness.
Your...
...Happiness.
Your...
...LO❤E!
It's all...
...In your HEAD!

"In your head, in your head
Zombie, zombie, zombie-ie-ie
What's in your head, in your head?
Zombie, zombie, zombie-ie-ie-ie, oh.

With their tanks and their bombs
And their bombs and their guns
In your head, in your head, they are crying

Zombie, zombie, zombie-ie-ie
What's in your head, in your head?
Zombie, zombie, zombie-ie-ie-ie, oh

Do, do, do, do
Do, do, do, do."

-*"Zombie" - "The Cranberries"*

"The Don"
05.12.2022

Heavy Rider

(Cavaliere Pesante)

You've heard of the *"Easy Rider"*...
...well, I'm not him!
I've got *a weight on my back.*
I've got *things going in my head.*
I've got *gravity weighing me down.*
Cause...
...*I'm the "Heavy Rider".*

I don't *travel light.*
I *take my shit with me.*
I don't *leave anyone behind.*
I don't *leave anything behind.*
I *take it all with me.*
Cause...
...*I'm the "Heavy Rider".*

I travel slow.
But I have places to go.
Things to do.
But I can't go any faster.
I'm tethered to the ground.
Cause...
...*I'm the "Heavy Rider".*

"The Don"
07.12.2022

Scream in the Night

(Grido nella notte)

07.12.2022

You *laugh.*
You *cry.*
You *sing.*
You *dance.*
You *yell.*
You *scream.*

But is there anyone out there?
Is there anyone listening?
Does anyone hear you?
Does anyone care?
When you scream in the night?

"The Don"
07.12.2022

Counter-Intuitive

(Controintuitivo)

It feels wrong.
It seems illogiçal.
You think you should be doing the opposite.
But somehow you KNOW it's the *"right"* thing to do.
It seems *"Counter-Intuitive"*.

You must go against the grain.
Swim against the tide.
Swim upstream.
Take the hard road.
Walk the rocky path.
Even though it seems *"Counter-Intuitive"*.

You know it's right.
You know it deep inside you.
Deep in your gut.
You know it's not logical.
You know that it's *"Counter-Intuitive"*.

"The Don"
07.08.2022

Everyone wants a new *adventure*.
Everyone wants a new *scene*.
Everyone wants a new *experience*.
Everyone wants a new *LO♥ER*.
Everyone wants a new *Romance*.

Everyone wants a new *job*.
Everyone wants a new *government*.
Everyone wants a new *society*.
Everyone wants a new *world*.
Everyone wants a new *planet*.
Everyone wants a new *life*.
Everyone wants a new *LO♥ER*.
Everyone wants a new *Romance*.

"Everybody's working for the weekend
Everybody wants a new romance
Everybody's goin' off the deep end
Everybody needs a second chance, oh
You want a piece of my heart
You better start from the start
You wanna be in the show
Come on baby let's go."

-"Everybody's working for the weekend" – "Loveboy"

"The Don"
13.12.2022

The Fun Had Gone

(Il Divertimento era Finito)

It had become tedious.
Doing the same old thing.
It had become boring.
Doing the same repetitions.
It had become repetitive.
Doing the same old *"shit"*.
It had become old.
The fun had gone.

It was over.
There was nothing new here.
Nothing new was going to happen.
It was just *"inertia"*.
There are many reasons for this.
I won't go into them.
But I'm sure you know what I'm talking about…
…the fun had gone.
It was time to move on.
Because...
…the fun had gone.

"The fun had gone
The fun had gone away
The fun had gone baby
The fun had gone away
You know you done me wrong baby
And you'll be sorry someday."

-based on the song, "The Thrill has Gone – "B.B. King"

"The Don"
15.12.2022

Learning

(Imparare)

I'm learning.
But it's a slow process.
This learning business.
I make mistakes.
I keep repeating the same mistakes...
...over & over again.
Surely, I must be learning from all this repetition.
Maybe I have a *"testa dura"*, a *"hard head"* in Italian?
When will I EVER learn?
Will I EVER learn?
Maybe not!
This learning thing is hard.
But I can't give up now.
I shouldn't give up now.
I must keep on trying...
...to keep learning!

"I'm learning to fly
But I ain't got wings
Coming down
Is the hardest thing.

I'm learning to fly.

I'm learning to fly.
But I ain't got wings"

-*"Learning to Fly" – "Tom Petty"*

"The Don"
16.12.2022

Down Low

(Giù in Basso)

I'm in a *rut*.
I'm in a *hole*.
I'm not *going anywhere*.
I'm not *doing anything*.
I'm in a *low*.
I'm *going down*.

"Down, down, deeper & down!
Down, down, deeper & down!
Deep down, deeper & down.
Stay down, stay on the ground.
I'm going down, deep & down.
Way down, down below the ground.
Down down, where I'll never be found."

-"Down, Down, Deeper & Down: - "Status Quo"

"The Don"
17.12.2022

(Devi Prendere AMORE Quando Puoi)

Don't be so *choosie*.
Don't be so *picky*.
Don't be so *exclusive*.
Don't be so *"high fullootin"*.
You gotta take LO❤E when you can.

You might not get a *second chance*.
You might not get *another offer*.
You might not get *"Lucky" next time*.
You might not even get to be *alive next time around*.
So...
...you gotta take LO❤E when you can.

There might not even be a *"next time"*!
So...
... you gotta take LO❤E when you can.

"If you can't be with the one you love,
Love the one you're with
Love the one you're with
Love the one you're with
Love the one you're with."

-"If you Can't be with the One you Love" – C,S & N

"The Don"
17.12.2022

Dead Man Walking

(Morto che Cammina)

I'm *talking.*
I'm *breathing.*
I'm *thinking.*
I'm *feeling.*
But....
...I'm a dead man walking.

She killed me.
She stabbed me in the heart.
She plunged the knife deep.
It went in very deep.
I didn't have a chance.
It was a fatal blow.
It was meant to kill.
And she didn't miss.
She didn't flinch.
She stared me right in the eyes...
...and drove the dagger into me.
...and twisted it.
...just to make sure I was dead.
And now...
...I'm a dead man walking.

"Dead man, dead man
When will you arise?
Cobwebs in your mind
Dust upon your eyes."

-"Dead Man, Dead Man" - "Bob Dylan"

"The Don"
18.12 2022

I Talk to Myself

(Parlo con me Stesso)

Am I *"Normal"*?
Is this ok?
Or...
...am I CRAZY?
Even...
..."*Mad*", maybe?
Because...
...*I talk to myself!*

How about you?
Do you talk to yourself?

"I talk too much,
I talk too much,
Even though I've got nothing to say.
If I keep on talking baby....
...I'll even talk to myself!"

"You Talk Too Much" – "George Thorogood & The Destroyers"

"The Don"
19.12.2022

All You Want is Sex

(Tutto quello che vuoi è il Sesso)

"All you want is sex!"
That's what she said.
Which got me thinking...
...is that all I want?
No, it's not all I want.
I want more.
Sex by itself is empty...
...meaningless.
I want more than just sex.
I want *affection*.
I want *intimacy*.
I want *friendship*.
I want *involvement*.
I want a *connection*.
I want a *relationship*.
I want *to be wanted*.
I want *LO*♥*E*.
I want to be *LO*♥*ED*.
That's what I want.
I DON"T want JUST sex.
Just to make everything clear.
Sex alone is not enough.
It is not satisfying.
It is not complete.

"I'm a sex bomb, sex bomb.
And baby, I can turn you on!
Sex bomb, sex bomb.
I'm a sex bomb.
And baby I can you on!"

-*"Sex Bomb"*
-*Writers: Nicole Hughes/Jeff Dalziel/Mark Holman*
-*Performed by: Tom Jones*

"The Don"
20.12.2022

Consumed by Nature

(Consumato dalla Natura)

Consumed by Nature.
That's how I want to go.
Enveloped in her hands.
Cocooned in her warmth.
Wrapped in her LO❤E.
Cradled by her security.
Surrounded by her progeny.
Entwined in her World.
Consumed by her Energy.
Transformed in her.
Her & I are as One.
We become One.
One Unity of Existence.
This is how I went to end up.
To *"shuffle if my mortal coil!"*
To be...
...consumed by Nature!

"I'd rather be a sparrow than a snail
Yes, I would
If I could
I surely would.

I'd rather be a hammer than a nail
Yes, I would
If I only could
I surely would.

Away, I'd rather sail away
Like a swan that's here and gone
A man gets tied up to the ground
He gives the world its saddest sound
Its saddest sound.

I'd rather be a forest than a street
Yes, I would
If I could
I surely would."

-"El Condor Pasa"
Written by: Daniel Alomia Robles/Paul Simon
Performed by: Simon & Garfunkel

"The Don"
21.12.2022

You Confuse Sex With LO❤E

(Confondi il Sesso con l'Amore)

You confuse sex with LOVE.
You don't use your vagina to find LOVE.
You use your HE❤RT.
Two completely different organs!

"The Don"
24.12.2022

You Gave Me Enough to Last Me a Lifetime

(Mi hai Dato Abbastanza per Durare Una Vita)

You gave me enough material to last me a lifetime!
You are FANTASTIC!
Thanks for that!

"The Don"
24.23.2022

Nick the Prick

(Nicolo il Coglione)

He's a *coward.*
He's *abusive.*
He's *bossy.*
He's *arrogant.*
He's *ignorant.*
He's *aggressive.*
He's *violent.*
He's *loud.*
He's an *arsehole.*
He's a *Fascist.*
He's a *hypocrite.*
He's a *"psycho"*!
He's Nick the prick!

One day he started *"bagging"* me out, in front of everybody.
It was Christmas day lunch...
...we hadn't even started the *"antipasto"*!
I lost it.
I let him have it.
I didn't hold back.
He can *"dish it out but he can't take it!"*
Because when you give it back to him...
...he can't take it!
He goes all CRAAAAAAZZZZZYYYY!
He'll run around like a *"headless chook!"*
Then he'll become contrite.
And he will apologise.
He's a prick.
He's...
... Nick the prick!
By the way...
...Nick is my brother!
Hahahaha!

"He's my brother
He ain't heavy, he's my brother
He ain't heavy, he's my brother."

_"He Ain't Heavy"-"The Hollies"

"The Don"
26.12 2022

Why Don't the Children Play?

(Perché i Bambini Non Giocano?)

It's TOO *HOT.*
It's TOO *COLD.*
It's *FLOODING.*
There is not enough *WATER.*
There is not enough *SPACE.*
The air is *POLLUTED.*
Why don't the children play?

There is too much *SOCIAL MEDIA.*
There is too much *AI (Artificial Intelligence).*
There is too much *INTERNET.*
There is *TERRORISM.*
There is *CIVIL UNREST.*
There is *FEAR on the streets.*
There is *CRUELTY.*
There is *INHUMANITY!*
Why don't the children play?

There is a *PLAGUE.*
There is a *CURFEW.*
There is *POLITICAL UNREST.*
There is *SOCIAL UNREST.*
There is *EXPLOITATION.*
There is *BRAIN-WASHING.*
There is a *corrupt POLITICAL SYSTEM.*
There is *POVERTY on the streets.*
There *ARE NO streets!!!!*
There is *CAPITALISM.*
Why don't the children play?

"That's why the children don't play!"

"I know we've come a long way
We're changing day to day
But tell me, why don't the children play?"

-*"Where Do the Children Play?"* – Cat Stevens

"The Don"
28.12.2022

I Fell in LO❤E With a Narcissist

(Mi Sono Innamorato di un Nacisista)

I fell in LO❤E with a *pianist*.
I fell in LO❤E with a *composer*.
I fell in LO❤E with a *"Player"*.
I fell in LO❤E with an *"Egoist"*.
I fell in LO❤E with a *"Bitch"*.
I fell in LO❤E with a *girl that "takes no prisoners"*.
I fell in LO❤E with a girl that *NEVER looks back*.
I fell in LO❤E with the girl with the *"large labia lips"*.
I fell in Machine with a *"Pleasure Machine"*.
I fell in LO❤E with a girl *whose parents wanted a "Boy"*.
I fell in LO❤E with a girl *who wanted to be a "Man"*.
I fell in LO❤E with a girl *that confused LO❤E with "Sex"*.
I fell in LO❤E with a girl *that didn't LO❤E "Me"*.
I fell in LO   E with a girl that *didn't find me "Sexually attractive"*.
I fell in LO❤E with a *"Braziliana"*.
I fell in LO❤E with *"The Girl from Ipanema"*.
I fell in LO❤E with a "NARCISSIST"!

"Tall and tan and young and lovely
The girl from Ipanema goes walking
And when she passes
Each one she passes goes, "Ah".

Oh, but he watches her so sadly
How can he tell her he loves her?
Yes, he would give his heart gladly
But each day, when she walks to the sea
She looks straight ahead, not at me.

But she doesn't see
She just doesn't see
No, she doesn't see
But she doesn't see
She doesn't see
No, she doesn't see."

-"The Girl From Ipanema" – Antonio Carlos Jobim

"The Don"
29.12.2022

It's Not Ok

(Non va Bene)

"Just remember..."
..."It's not ok to not be ok?"

"Did you mean, *"It's ok to be not ok."*
Or...
Did you mean, *"It's not ok to be ok?"*
Or...
..."It's ok to be ok?"
Or...
..."It's not to be not ok, to be not ok?"
Or...
... "It's not ok to be not ok, not ok?"

"Wait on!"
"Wait on!"
"Can you repeat that?
"Sure!
"It's not ok to not be ok?"
Did you mean, *"It's not ok to be ok?"*
Or...
..."It's ok to not be ok?"
Or...
..."It's ok to be ok?"
Or...
..."It's not to be not ok, to be not ok?"
Or...
... "It's not ok to be not ok, not ok?"

"Now I'm REALLY confused."
"What don't you understand?"
"Pretty clear to me!"
"Yeah, as clear as mud!"
"Ok, now I have to shoot you!..."
..."with my harmonica!"

"The Don"
30.12.2022

The Dying of the Light

(Il Morire della Luce)

"The Don"
30.12.2022

Do NOT let the *"DARKNESS"* win!

Because We Die, We Have Time

(Perché Moriamo, Abbiamo Tempo)

It's ALL about *MORTALITY.*
It's all about *DEATH.*
Our DEATH!
Because we DIE...
...we have TIME!

If we didn't die...
If we were immortal...
Then there would be no need for time.
Time would be irrelevant.
But because we DIE.
...we have TIME!

Time is conceived to measure our life.
From our birth to our death.
We are always conscious of it.
We cannot escape it.
It's because we DIE...
...that we have TIME!

"Ticking away the moments that make up a dull day
Fritter and waste the hours in an offhand way
Kicking around on a piece of ground in your hometown
Waiting for someone or something to show you the way.

Every year is getting shorter, never seem to find the time
Plans that either come to naught or half a page of scribbled lines
Hanging on in quiet desperation is the English way
The time is gone, the song is over, thought I'd something more to say."

-"Time"
Written by: Roger Waters
Performed by: Pink Floyd

"The Don"
03.01 2023

Faster than Lager Turns to Piss

(Più Veloce di Lager si Trasforma in Piscio)

*What the FUCK does this
actually mean?*
I mean it's DEFINITELY true.
There is no TRUER statement.
Lager definitely turns to piss very quickly!
FUCK!
I REALLY hate that!
The Lager has become piss!
It's undrinkable!
I have to force myself.
And the schooner is still 3/4 full!
FUCK!
It's a REAL torture!
I'm REALLY suffering!

I'll think I'll get a G&T next!

"The Don"
05.01.2023

Turd on the Run

(Stronzo in Fuga)

How Many Times Can You Polish Up a Turd?
You can't polish up a turd.
It'll always be a turd.
Once a turd always a turd.
It's a turd on the run.

You can dress it up in fancy clothes.
Make it wear a suit & tie.
You can send it to school.
You can spray it with *"Eu de Colone".*
But...
...once a turd.
...always a turd.
That's just the *"Nature"* of turds.

"I don't wanna know your name
'Cause you don't look the same
The way you did before
Okay, you think you got a pretty face
But the rest of you is out of place
You looked alright before.

Turd on the run
You scream and everybody comes.
Take a run and hide yourself away
The turd is on the run.

Turd on the run
You scream and everybody comes.
Take a run and hide yourself away
The turd is on the run."

- *"Fox on the Run" – The Sweet*

"The Don"
03.01.2023

Desolation Road

(Strada della Desolazione)

There are so many roads.
There's...
...*Tobacco Road.*
...*Copperhead Road.*
...*Telegraph Road.*
...*Highway 61.*
...*Route 66.*
...*Stairway to Heaven.*
...*Highway Star.*
...*The Yellowbrick Road.*
...*The Long & Winding Road.*
...*The Lost Highway.*
...*Highway to Hell.*
...*Road to Nowhere.*
...The Road that leads you to my HEART.
Which one will you choose?
Be careful?
Don't make the wrong choice.
Take your time.
Don't rush your decision.
Don't panic.
But whatever you do don't choose...
...*Desolation Road!*

It's a vast empty road.
You'll see no one.
You'll hear nothing.
It's completely empty.
Devoid of all life!
It's where your demons travel.
Whatever you do...
...*don't go along Desolation Road.*

You won't like who you meet.
You won't like what you see.
You won't like what you hear.
You'll meet traitors.
You'll see visions.
You'll hear voices.
Out on...
...Desolation Road.

"They're selling postcards of the hanging
They're painting the passports brown
The beauty parlor is filled with sailors
The circus is in town
Here comes the blind commissioner
They've got him in a trance
One hand is tied to the tight-rope walker
The other is in his pants
And the riot squad they're restless
They need somewhere to go
As Lady and I look out tonight
From Desolation Row."

- "Desolation Row" – Bob Dylan

"The Don"
04.01.2023

I'm the Man that Put the Bang into Gang

(Sono l'Uomo che ha Messo il Bang in Gang)

I'm the man that put the bang in gang!

-*"Wanna Be in My Gang?" – Garry Glitter*

I'm the Man that Put the Bang into Gang

(Sono l'Uomo che ha Messo il Bang in Gang)

"The Don
06.01.2023

No Chains Around My Feet

(Nessuna Catena Intorno ai Miei Piedi)

There are no chains around my feet but I am NOT free!

-"Concrete Jungle" – Bob Marley

"The Don"
06.01.2023

I am Sixty-Four

(Ho Sessantaquattro Anni)

I should know more.
More than before.
But do I?
I don't think so!
In fact, I think I know less.
I think I know SHIT!
I know NOTHING!
So, what have I learnt?
I've learned a LOT!
And I'll tell you what I've learnt...
... that I know NOTHING at all!
Now that I'm Sixty-four.

I'm older.
I'm bolder.
I have NO FEARS.
I'm a terrior!
NOTHING can STOP meeeeee!!!
I'm INVINCIBLE!
I'm a FORCE to be reckoned with.
I'm a FORCE of NATURE!
Now that I'm Sixty-four.

But what's it all for?
Now that I'm Sixty-four.

"When I get older losing my hair
Many years from now
Will you still be sending me a Valentine
Birthday greetings bottle of wine
If I'd been out till quarter to three
Would you lock the door?

Will you still need me?
Will you still feed me?
When I'm sixty-four?"

- "When I'm Sixty-Four" – Lennon & McCartney

"The Don"
13 01.2023

I'm Only Human

(Sono Solo Umano)

I am not to blame.
It's not my fault.
I didn't do it.
I know you've heard that before.
But that's my defence.
My ONLY defence.
I did my best.
I tried my hardest.
I put my HE❤RT & SOUL into it.
I gave it ALL I had!
I gave it my *"A -Game"*.
I left nothing in the tank.
I was empty.
I was exhausted.
I was defeated.
I was a FAILURE!
But...
...*I'm only Human.*

"I'm only human
I'm only, I'm only
I'm only human, human.

Maybe I'm foolish
Maybe I'm blind
Thinking I can see through this
And see what's behind
Got no way to prove it
So maybe I'm blind.

But I'm only human after all
I'm only human after all
Don't put your blame on me
Don't put your blame on me.

But I'm only human after all
I'm only human after all"

-"Human" – Rag'n'Bone Man

"The Don"
15.01.2023

I CAN'T PROTECT YOU

(Non Posso Proteggerti)

Whenever someone says to you that...
..."I can protect you!"
Don't listen to them.
Definitely, do NOT believe them.
They are PREDATORS!
What they are actually saying is...
"...I'm a PREDATOR!"
"...I'm a user!"
"...I'm an abuser!"
"...I will exploite you!"
"...I will treat you like an object!"
"...I will DEHUMANISE you!
"...I POSSESS you!"
"...I will OWN you!"
"...I will CONTROL you!"
"...I might even TERRORISE you!"

So, whenever someone says to you that...
..."I can protect you!"
Do NOT believe them.
Actually, you need protection from THEM!
So...
...RUN away!
As FAST as you can!

"The Don"
15.01.2023

Books written by "The Don"

"Poems for ALIENS, Outsiders, Outcasts & other STRANGE BEINGS!"
Published: 10th April, 2021
Book of Poems 9

"Poems for Beings From Another Planet"
Published: 10th May, 2021
Book of Poems 10

"Poems for Mindless Beings & Lost Souls"
Published: 10th June, 2021
Book of Poems 11

"Poems for the Broken Hearted & Misunderstood
Published: 10th July, 2021
Book of Poems 12

"Poems for Poems for the Bewildered, Dazed & Confused"
10th August, 2021

Book of Poems 13

"Poems for the Outsiders, Displaced, Dispossessed, Discarded & Unwanted"
Published: 10th Sept, 2021
Book of Poems 14

All available ONLY online

"Poems for Secret Agents, Phantom Agents, Agents of Change, Agent Provocateurs & Agents of Chaos"
Published: 10th Oct, 2021

Book of Poems 15

"Poems for Disenchanted, Disillusioned & Delusional"
Published: 10th November, 2021
Book of Poems 16

Books written by "The Don"

"Poems for the Stoners, drugos, ACID takers & Psychedelic LO❤ERS (Everybody Must Get Stoned)"
Published: 10th December, 2021
Book of Poems 17

"Poems for Anarchists, Rebels & Revolutionaries
Published: 10th January, 2022
Book of Poems 18

"Poems for Rebels, Radicals & Revolutionaries (Viva la Révolution!)"
Published: 10th February, 2022
Book of Poems 19

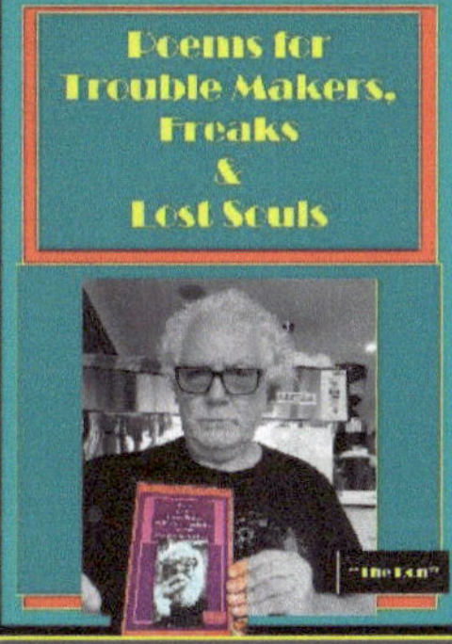

"Poems for Trouble Makers, Freaks & Lost Souls"
Published: 10th March 2022
Book of Poems 20

"Poems for Zombies & the Walking Dead"
Published: 10th April 2022
Book of Poems 21

"Poems for Non-Conformists (Never conform!)"
Published: 10th May 2022
Book of Poems 22

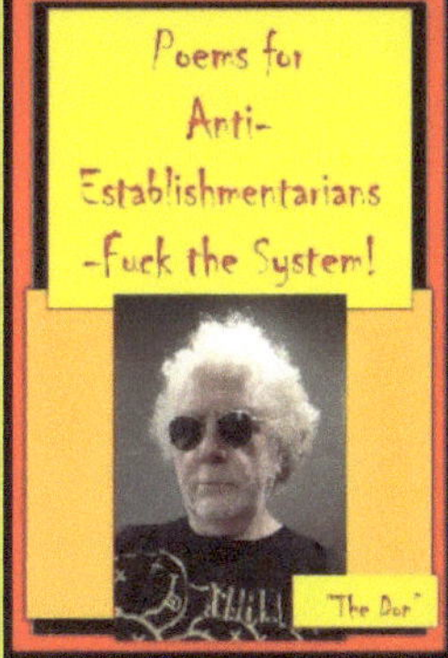

"Poems for Anti-Establishment-arians -Fuck the System!"
Published: 10th June 2022
Book of Poems 23

"Poems for the Voiceless"
Published: 10th July 2022
Book of Poems 24

All available ONLY online

www.ingramcontent.com/pod-product-compliance
Lightning Source LLC
Chambersburg PA
CBHW041232050726
47599CB00007B/919

CONTENTS

"Forever Young"

"May you grow up to be righteous
May you grow up to be true
May you always know the truth
And see the light surrounding you
May you always be courageous
Stand upright and be strong
May you stay forever young
May you stay forever young."

"May your hands always be busy
May your feet always be swift
May you have a strong foundation
When the winds of changes shift
May your heart always be joyful
May your song always be sung
And may you stay forever young
May you stay forever young."

-Bob Dylan